Désarroi

Poems by T.L. Pompey

ISBN: 9798665093680

Cover Photo by
Markus Spiske
www.markusspiske.com
Courtesy of Unsplash.com

The author wishes to acknowledge the following publications:

Art/Life for "Chickamauga Revisited"
California State Poetry Quarterly for "Casual Dinner Conversation"
Daybreak for "Looking at Drawings of Prehistoric Man"
Medicinal Purposes Literary Review for "Warning Light"
BorderSenses for "Mass Transit"

for Doris
who read it all
and still remained cheerful

Contents

I thought to myself, "Look, I have grown and
increased in wisdom more than anyone who has
ruled over Jerusalem before me; I have
experienced much of wisdom and knowledge."
Then I applied myself to the understanding of
wisdom, and also of madness and folly, but I
learned that this, too, is a chasing after the wind.

For with much wisdom comes much sorrow;
the more knowledge, the more grief.
Ecclesiastes 1:16-18

SOLOMON PAUSES IN HIS LIBRARY

There was a moment
when I had her by my fingertips.
Nothing more than a coattail
but still, I was riding.

A seesaw affair to be sure,
highs and lows and plenty
of broken bones, yet days
when I sensed simpatia.

I let her go, reluctantly,
after long hard thought.
Not because I lost sight.
No, to this day
she remains clearly in view.

Rather, she would not speak
and I grew tired of us living like
dried-up lovers with nothing left to say.

Occasionally we eye each other,
competing cats with tails twitching,
poised for a good fight,
secretly preferring to run away.

LEAVING THE PROMISED LAND

"I will stand there before you by the rock at Horeb.
Strike the rock, and water will come out of it for the people to drink."
So Moses did this in the sight of the elders of Israel.

Exodus 17:6

I have come to Horeb, thirsty as
an Israelite. Not compelled by Moses,
but freely to the rock, as if by simply
standing here, I could squeeze from
this desert stone one last drop. Such
the risk of pilgrimage. Moses gone.
Mouth dry. Mountain staring back.

THE PHYSICS OF FAITH

There is a time to stop believing.
Like power brakes hit forcefully.
Like a bullet to the chest.

You cannot sustain faith.
The laws of nature prove it:
that friction creates resistance,
that systems disintegrate,
that gravity pulls everything back.

So, for the idealist and revolutionary,
the poet and preacher, a time to cease:
to sink down and settle
in patterns among fish and flora;
to let motion carry us
wherever it pleases;
to wake up after a vivid dream
and discover with relief
it's just an ordinary day.

THE LONG RUN

Whatever your destiny, that dream you work for,
what is it exactly?

Frank, for instance, did the right thing, worked hard,
kept his garden neat, always greeted neighbors.
His goal was retirement.

Now he sits quietly in his chair, gone from Alzheimer's.
This is not what we planned his wife grieves.

No, I agree, but we pursue our plans relentlessly
and that is our conundrum.

A MAN APPEARING AS ME

Just when my feet get firmly planted,
the earth shifts and throws me off.
Some people do not have this problem.
They look at me with unblinking eyes
and I assume: They know something I don't.
Then the earth shifts again
and my body teeter-totters.

The artist knows what I can't verbalize.
There is life wafting unseen,
shape-shifting like a Hopi legend.
Here I am at this moment appearing
as a man on the street.
I will close my eyes and sleep.
When I wake, you will not even notice
I am someone else.

BIOLOGY LESSON

A tree appears to be still. In fact,
it's as busy as New York, growing
and decaying simultaneously,
as I am — but who can tell just by looking?

So much science broods unseen.
I often calculate backwards to catch
what I've missed but simple reason
is not enough. A tree's soul is buried
in its roots. Try as you might,
you cannot find it, even with a shovel.

MAPPA MUNDI, HEREFORD CATHEDRAL

In 1280 scholars believed
this was the world;
paradise on top,
Jerusalem the center,
the rest all legends
linked like a jigsaw.

We have had years
to sort this out.
The best scientists.
The finest philosophers.
The renaissance has come
and gone and come again.

As for the new Mundi —
fresh continents,
knowledge as high priest,
Jerusalem independent,
all re-vamped and still
no closer to paradise.

FILM FOOTAGE OF THE *TITANIC*

On the bottom of the Atlantic,
twelve-thousand feet deep,
the wreckage remains,

steel, wood and glass,
walls, pipes, and doors,
still recognizable as a ship,

human ingenuity at its best,
resting comfortably during
hubris and decadence,
war and genocide.

Not a soul in sight.
It is a deserted city,
a graveyard without crypts.

We are so good with monuments,
these loving, brutal tributes
that finally become sacred
after we perish.

THE BIG BANG

It still happens. Hiroshima. The Beatles. Cell phones.
9/11. Lately I've become aware how the frequency has increased.
The tempo of the song picking up. The drums louder. The flashing
lights more severe.

What I've set in motion has now turned to face me. The booms
of something approaching — an army, a firestorm, or simply my own
noise. The thunder and wind are picking up. The rifles fire
and the ice melts. Odd how, when I look around, it all seems
so matter-of-fact, as if I expect it, but not before dinner.

This is the nature of the Big Bang. Normal. Harsh. Bodies
scattered. Cities lost. Forests burned. And always the question,
like the dinosaurs' descendants: Who will survive to notice?

CASUAL DINNER CONVERSATION

If I said to you
over peppered steak
A soul exists as broken glass
you would sip your wine calmly
and reply
The world is what my eyes tell me.
True enough.
If you could see a menu of the world
you would know.
First a gash
then a hemorrhage
then a tourniquet.
Rubbish
you would laugh
with bread buttered,
Utterly morose rubbish.
Then I would write in big letters
on our freshly laundered table cloth
A soul exists as broken glass
and as you dropped your fork,
you would finally notice
on my hands and yours,
fresh cuts.

EATING LUNCH AT MING DYNASTY

Sipping water, I see,
on surrounding walls
Oriental calligraphy
with cryptic messages
for the wise and observant.
I sit and stare at them as if
everything I've known
about love and life remains
profoundly Chinese.

FOR JAMES AND LEO

In the spring of '71 on a small country highway,
James and Leo, two guys just out of high school,
drunk and speeding, wrapped their car around a tree.
Both gone in a flash and a puff of smoke.

We all duly noted the wages of sin and moved on.

Today I'm driving Highway 101 weaving my way
to work. James and Leo cross my mind
as Springsteen sings *Wreck on the Highway*.
I realize I'm moving just as fast and sin
has yet to pay me.

Tomorrow or today, perhaps James and Leo
will visit with check in hand and a smirk
as if they knew all along I'd pass them
in the fast lane.

WHAT DEBBIE TAUGHT ME

On a hot spring day
at the end of term,
without her normal
jocks or groupies
to embarrass me,
I screw up my courage
and ask her out.

As expected, she smiles
and politely says no.

This is the lesson
I have learned:
You dream, you die,
and sometimes
you can't tell the difference.

ADDICT

A man needs love
like food and water
and I need more than most,
constantly digging for new sources,
knowing what I want
is in limited supply.

It is a passionate world
but not tender.
Some pay for love.
Others are resigned.
I was born to hunt for it
with radar and anger
and bulldog persistence.

And it will kill me,
as certain as I breathe,
pawing as I have for it
in cracks and corners,
a wino, stuporous,
looking for his bottle,
believing like all derelicts
that somewhere in my lifetime
there must be enough.

BABY TUCKED AWAY IN A RESTAURANT

I am surprised to think:
a year ago baby was not here.

Who says the universe is closed?
While I worked and slept, oblivious,
this man and woman conceived.

Birth is our fate and power.
Pent up passion and circumstance.
Deliberate desire and raw chance.
The casino of our thighs
gambling the world's history.
We are nothing without risk.

Baby and I sit calmly watching.
They order their food and wait
for the cards to be dealt.

MASS TRANSIT

I board the 6A at C and Robert,
pay my fare, and blend in.

The American dream here is quite dry.
One soul brother mumbles as he gets off:
Ain't no black ever gonna be president.

The ride has taught me how silly I've been
complaining and making so much noise.
No more wasted motion. Just journey.

This is how I view my commute.
This is how I view my life.
The act of existence — simple enough.

I board, I ride, I get off: short, undramatic.
For all my fuss and haste, I remain a rider
on a fixed schedule, arriving and leaving
through the side door like a quick gust.

The bus roars off. The passengers remain
transfixed.

PICTURES OF ELLIS ISLAND, ca. 1910

What did we promise these poor people?
What did we promise ourselves?

Life, liberty, the pursuit of . . .

Like an ad in a magazine.
A bit of truth. A lot of sale.

You may believe in the idea
but the heart is not a mirror.
There remains much unseen.

Like these immigrants,
I believed but I cannot
promise anything in return,
not to them or myself,
not anymore.

They still come for the money
but liberty is more fragile.

We have all tried wearing her glass slipper
on many occasions
and felt it shatter.

HALF AWAKE

There is to living a certain inevitability,
palatable with justice or mercy
but what to do when you believe
and yet not and hope and yet not.
Is it better to sleep and dream?
Is it better to dwell in the nightmare?

To wake up from your dream
and face the moment:
that is unbearable sadness,

like the boy who relishes
Christmas and Santa Claus
then learns the gift
and the wonder it brought
was only the wrapping;
that in his haste to believe,
he had, in fact, been duped.

TRAVELING BY GOLDEN GATE NATIONAL CEMETERY

A show of mythic proportions:
freedom, bravery, sacrifice,
neatly arranged across green hills
for families on their way
to the mall.

Tell us how you went willingly
and how, when the guns screamed,
your last thought was: *for my country.*

As for me, I am reduced
to counting tombstones.
Nothing I say
can help you speak frankly.

There is no arguing with the dead,
especially you, decorated,
precisely laid out, unable
to re-evaluate your politics
or utter any protest against
such a savage departure.

COPPER HILL

Back in the woods, off the main drag —
Copper Hill. Named for the obvious.
One of strip mining's little secrets.

At Copper Hill entire hillsides were blasted.
Laid up against surrounding forests,
a piece of post-nuclear landscape.

I passed by there many times headed for Georgia
and never got used to it. As if I'd found,
in the midst of Eden, the rot of temptation.

Those mines ate up the souls of folk who lived there.
They chewed on me as well but, like clothes shoved
under a bed, I could shut the door and forget.

Survival it's called. Don't waste time on what can't be changed
and as I travel through cities and states and points west,
I make sure Copper Hill always veers out of sight.

WARNING LIGHT

A few childhood events
hang in my head
like old snapshots
framed years ago,
undusted in my house.
For instance,
that weird green hall lamp
left on at night,
and the warning not to get up
because snakes crawled
on the floor.
I kept an eye out
as the lamp stared at me.
A lasting impression.
I believed every word.
I still do.

AMUSE THE BEAST

The ones in the show know:
the spinners and choreographers,
the dancers and jugglers,
the wordsters and picturists.
It's all about gullibility.

When did I surrender?
Perhaps quite young
when adults suckled me.
Perhaps later because
the slogans sounded good.

Somewhere backstage
I always trusted in a well.
Go down far enough,
bring a good flashlight,
you could find decent water.

I tell you folks the well,
if it existed, is bone dry.
In its place, a corps of chats
demanding information as if
it was a cure for cancer.

All the while, the gray beast —
there in the corner, half-hidden,
pointing a clawed finger at me.
Now, he nods, it's my turn
to lend support for
slippery-smooth acquiescence.

PRAYER

Prayer changes things I was taught as a child.
And again: *Persistence and prayer go hand-in-hand.*

For what reason, against what odds, I cannot tell you.
Every week I go to church. Every week the church prays.
Every week I go home wondering.

About Adam's walks with God. About Jesus' miracles.
About death and disease. About my own routine life.
About who is really listening: The Father as priest.
The Son as doctor. The Spirit as magician.

Today I sit on a park bench and look up into the sky,
one man among billions, hoping to hear something —
answers for this planet at war, starving, plotting, asleep —
as if the blue reflection is a prism channeling thought.
I pray that I might make sense of this, small sense,
enough to keep me looking through the glass.

It is a nice day, a perfect day for asking.
I wait patiently, like a good son, for a response.

COMMUTE, OXNARD TO SAN DIEGO

Los Angeles tips the world
out of balance.
Like a cyclops gone blind,
the weight and force
of his madness creates
a warped gyration.

Those of us in his path
tease the mammoth
but no one is safe.
Play with him long enough
and he will eat you.

Meanwhile the rest of the globe
flocks to watch the spectacle,
the sight of him dancing in circles
and growling like a circus bear,
proof that, deep in our brain,
blood and death,
live and in person,
are amusing.

E-MAIL

Every day I open my box.
Call it curiosity or necessity.
I don't care.

I need to see for myself
the great herd of hucksters
roaming underground like lost buffalo
waiting to stampede my bank account.

They know it. I know it. Desire
looking for its itch, constantly painting:
penis size, nakedness, sex, pills, real estate,
tsunamis of the human heart
cut up into snack-size kilobytes.

Chemical imbalance or hint of heaven?
Crack in my brain or peephole?
The marketeers roll it out.
I choose to delete or keep.

This is what it means to be human:
to hide in the garden with my secret knowledge,
to stay alert in case the voice of God
should ever come searching.

TRAFFIC REPORT

The molecules of our generation:
Cars. Built one by one, procreating.

Sparks, smoke, fire
burning itself to scraps.
The DNA, however, indestructible:

capable of being cloned
into other body parts, other children,
other large families.

Henry Ford could not have imagined this.
Here on the 101, 405, 5, 10,
strands upon strands writhing.

From the sky you can easily tell
what has been birthed:
an entire new species driving us.

KANSAS TRIPTYCH

I. Wind

Free to whip past
like a wraith
upending hairstyles
and patios,
scattering big rigs
and birds.

On whatever fence
you roost,
always the same demon
prowling the prairie
unrepentant.

Run for shelter
but do not think
you can escape.

II. Grass

Scattered for miles,
as plentiful as
Abraham's children.

There is a dozer
to my right
and a housing tract.

The sheaves crowd
the back yards
and wait.

Even if today we win,
tomorrow is theirs because,
as all prophets know,

the grass owns us.

III. Sky

Whatever you imagine
is mirrored —
freedom, judgment,
all other opinions.

You can only wonder
if old folk raised up
from either side
of the Missouri
wander the clouds
still arguing.

It is reassuring to know
when I talk to myself
the sky always listens.

VIDEO PARLOR

Our children here, faces absorbed
in the boom, the bass, the lights.
This is their paradise, their future.

I can't hear myself, can't even get them
to raise an eyebrow, they are
so primally stimulated.

Soon they will be adults, having learned
from years of practice how to press
buttons and get results,

how to move back and forth
among partners and destroy
whatever they please
without voicing a word.

PICK YOUR PART

I'm dispatching this morning for the world's largest
self-service auto recycler. Wrecks. Tows. Donations.
Sales of parts. Also, discretely, looking through the open
office window: wind blowing, sunshine, chlorophyl, pollen,
baby birds. Other partners in the business. A large raven
flies by to check our progress. So far, we are doing well:
half a dozen cars received, more scheduled tomorrow.
I consult with the giant, silent brain in the back office
of the universe who checks a ledger and nods. Today
at least, we are all on schedule.

NEST

Mother bird feeds her four babies with small bites.
They are all overshadowed by the roof,
the big blue sky, the clash of world events.
Jesus once observed how the Father knows about the sparrow.
Perhaps the whole Trinity is tuned in to watch this nest.
Perhaps they notice me also watching them watch.
Perhaps we are all aware at this moment
how small flocks of chicks can control the universe.

JACARANDA

Blooming like a Paris fashion run,
the Jacaranda dresses the epitome
of gorgeous — privileged, brilliant,
unafraid to shed clothes.

From a distance I'm impressed,
the same cross-eyed awe I have
meeting my favorite movie star.
Up close I see the careless smile,
the shortlivedness, the purple sap.

Standing beneath these branches,
I'm afraid to imagine because
I may actually get what I want,
that and all its attending luggage,
the clutter of loveliness, the excess
work it takes to clean up the mess.

QUICK GLANCES THROUGH THE WINDOW

1.   A plant is born with a plan,
grows without questions or grief,
watches me resist.

2.   There is night and day.
There is land and atmosphere.
There is me in the middle.

3.   Crow leans forward on a perch
but not far enough
to offer an opinion.

4.   Clouds waste no motion
and travel as directed.
Meanwhile I fight gravity.

5.   For anyone who looks up,
this giant fichus
offers an open womb.

FLATBEDS AND TOW TRUCKS

Every week on T.V. I patiently endure hundreds
of car commercials promising sex, success, and happiness.
Today I'm watching these wrecks being towed to the lot.

Every guarantee has a grey lining and needs to be
recycled. These are our fantasies being hauled in, cracked
and spoiled like old eggs.

Meanwhile, in board rooms and factories across
the world, new promises are being built and advertised
just to keep our spirits up.

ENDANGERED

I've always believed in Orangutans.
One of many truths I take for granted.
Like the existence of air, water, faith.

The Orangutans — disappearing.
Gone, perhaps, in my lifetime.
Only a picture to prop me up.
A small memory gone dormant,
as certainty curls itself to sleep.

DIAGRAM OF *DIMENSIONAL MAN*

Stripped down to the bare essentials,
bones and muscle standing on the top shelf
revealing all the layers that make up the body,
looking like a character from a B horror movie,
staring at me, his brother, rather sadly
asking for my help, my understanding.
As our eyes lock, I do not know if I can
help him or anybody else become more human.

LOOKING AT DRAWINGS OF PREHISTORIC MAN

Suppose Neanderthal discovered
more than wheels and fire.
Suppose he knew by his sharp sense
where to find both food and God.
Suppose he was born with keen intelligence
and we by sheer determination
have managed to dull ourselves.
Suppose he could see us now
from his privileged perspective
our faces like pictures in a book.
Would he recognize us?

FOUNDATION CRACK

The concrete floor in my church is cracked.
Some underground force has pushed through,
a seismic dragon digging up.

I am immediately concerned:
about God's protection and the daily struggles
above and below ground.

I check the walls, the girders, and ask how long
they can last against angels and demons
pounding the frame.

I am always on guard against the obvious.
Nothing loud ever comes through the front.
It is always the silence that sneaks up on me
and delivers the punch.

Here, while I listen and sing or sleep,
something strong slips underneath.
Here as I sit and rub my foot across the rift,
I wonder if my faith could repair this
and if I could defend myself
should the dragon finally crawl out.

RESTAURANT IN FLORIDA

The South is unkind to its daughters.
Owled eyes waiting on me speak
of hard work and sleepless nights.

> *Can I help you?* she asks in her smoker's voice
> but the weight of speaking caves in her mouth
> and I'm afraid my reply will make her face collapse.

BABES AT THE SANDWICH FACTORY

Two pretty young girls drive up in a late-model
sparkling blue Mustang convertible and walk
into the sandwich joint where I'm eating.
Early twenties, dressed breezily, smiling.
It appears fun is on their minds. With a car
and bodies like that, why not?

I try to remember if I've ever had that much fun.
It's a fickle emotion subject to the whims of some
invisible finger that picks and chooses without
rationale. I can't recall. Perhaps many years,
college or before, since I woke up feeling loose
and determined that today I'm going to laugh
and drive and do nothing important.

I finish my sandwich and think about work.
Important but not fun. I'm not sure I can expect
fun again, if it's even fair to ask. The sun shines
beautifully as I pull out of the parking lot.
My stereo is blasting. The invisible finger floats
over my head and spins roulette.

RESTAURANT AQUARIUM

The fish in the tank swim somberly
up and down inside their water prison
looking at me quizzically as if I
(or someone else eating) should speak.

I don't know what to say. I'm sure
at some point, when fish and men
were more similar, we might have
conversed, our evolutionary bodies
allowing us to swim peaceably together.

Now, however, we are both trapped,
locked out on two sides of a thin wall.

So much energy in this universe wasted,
deflected and bouncing in useless circles
while through clear plates fish and men
look at each other, mouths moving,
but not a single clear syllable.

All through the meal we eye each other
thinking the glass might break.

28 YEARS AGO TODAY

I graduated from college. Walked down the aisle
like an arrogant little prick whose future was wide open.
Knew nothing about survival or luck. Thought somehow,
between God and me, things would fall into place
and my life would be noted for its specialness.
That is, after all, what I grew up with — evangelical,
personal relationship with Jesus, one of God's lambs.
I wanted to be a preacher or teacher and I was pretty sure,
as I put on my gown, if I could get through this damned graduation,
the next day I would head for Colorado and get on with the show.
Didn't think much about a plan. Didn't care much for detail.
Didn't think when I said goodbye to Sheila she would cry.
Didn't realize when I left home I wasn't coming back.
You don't take in all of this when you're in a hurry.
It was me and my diploma and a beat-up Volkswagen.
Sayonara.

Of course I was young for a reason:

To get the hell beat out of me. To wake up one morning,
twenty-eight years later, and be thankful to be alive.
To see the complexity of the human race staring
me in the face and realize that God and I live together
as force fields, colliding, co-habitating, falling apart.
Mercurial, quiet, mysterious, off-setting.

I now assume my micro-place in the world. Older. Humbled.
Not quite a prick, I'll walk down the aisle of a restaurant tonight,
have dinner with my wife, and tell her I love her. I've thrown out
the sonofabitch who wants to be a preacher-teacher and gotten on
with the bits and pieces of my work, whatever it was God intended.
And here I'll remain as one human being in a very opaque world
blissfully adrift and floating in normalness.

ENTROPY

I.

Letting go of you was the hardest,
more so in that you found it so easy
to let go of me,

like an old bill in a drawer
or a shirt to a thrift store.

These straps I'm born with
have all frayed and broken
and still I outlive them

yet I'm clinging to you
by the thinnest of strands
waiting for the last ping.

That sound will be the cruelest,
the irretrievable swish of a ghost.

How inevitable this is that two
people fighting for independence
would readily give each other up.

I am not sorry, only stung and numbed
by how right it feels to unloose you.

II.

As for you my dear,
I'm willing to take the hit.
I was a pup and should have been older.
I was older and should have been smarter.
Such is the mess a man can make.

Each moment I live gets frozen
and no amount of begging can thaw it.
Live long enough and your life
becomes an iceberg

Here I am, moored in open sea,
next to your disbelief.
I imagine this is my debt
visible to ships for miles.

I'm moving slowly by inches
away from you, my feet clamped,
still accumulating ice as I calculate
how heavy it will be,
what a crashing sound it will make
when my floe finally breaks apart.

III.

I was recruited and raised for purity.
Where it went wrong, I cannot say.
Bad genes, bad karma, who knows?

The bond of a soldier is thick
but here we are split apart.
Serving in the same army,
not even God could hold us.

How ironic that as soldiers
we have both fled our posts
and run off into the night
not even recalling the basics,

acting like footloose privates
without commanders,
without cause,
without compassion,

while the enemy poses,
confident and reassuring,
as our diplomat.

IV.

Both of you died in nursing homes.
Quickly. Efficiently. Without fuss.
I was miles away and no comfort.
A son without kinship.

> *This is the nature of life and death.*
> *To provide order and transition.*
> *To cause grief and loss.*
> *To swallow up protest.*

I was not aware of your final thoughts.
Whether or not you asked for me.
Whether conscious or unconscious
you thought I'd come and say goodbye.

> *This is the nature of life and death.*
> *To break apart large into small.*
> *To sort us into byproducts.*
> *To limit our faith.*

It unnerves me that you died alone
but you were already isolated.
Even if I came, I'm not sure
I could have bridged the gap.

> *This is the nature of life and death.*
> *To give time then remove it.*
> *To lure us into stupor.*
> *To sneak up and remove our souls.*

Life was not kind to us.
Even less so death.
Only the steady drip of sedation
can relax our resistance.

This is the nature of life and death.
To create a false sense of destiny.
To push us into the universe.
To play hide-and-seek from the other side.

CASINO NIGHT, POST-PROM PARTY

They play my Wheel of Fortune
with frivolous abandon.
Teenagers, still strong at 3 AM.
The real wheel hasn't hit them yet
and I don't have the heart to tell them.
Chips on the table, they holler
like cheerleaders and with each loss
immediately bounce back.

The human race is divided into two classes:
winners and losers.
Both require tremendous belief.

I cannot distinguish tonight who is who
and for the moment, it's irrelevant.
They have the eyes and I'm willing to play along.
Around and around until the chips
seem permanently stuck to their fingers.

I realize as I check my watch,
how tired my hands are,
how exhausting it is to keep spinning,
how anxious I am to finish the game.

TOUGH

As in I have to be. No alternative allowed.
Room for diversion but not softness.
Room for power but not sweetness.

Push hard and discover how I rely on myself
to sleep on my bed of nails without giving clue
that my soul is bleeding.

A man may laugh hearty but do not be fooled.
There is always this thing lurking in his belly
out of sight —

lividity like the forest
underneath a fallen log,
life scurrying for cover.

Make him speak and you will see.
Oozing from a sore, a cut, or from his eyes,
what he keeps hidden: his own tenderness.

SHOPPING AT AMAR RANCH

Vegetables and fruits, different.
The language, Spanish.
Families comfortable.
Children shouting in the aisles.

Mothers, field-hands, and other
Latinos mix with a smattering
of Whites and Asians
around the produce.

In my house, the world is small.
Pictures of my family.
English books and magazines.

In this market it hits me.
Citizens and migrants
from points south,
glad to come here
and find home again.

Here in Amar's,
the nations gather,
serious and casual shoppers
sorting through piles
to find the best.

No one needs to speak
a word to understand
the delicacy of a good orange.

BREAKFAST AT MCDONALD'S

Their current marketing catch phrase — *I'm lovin' it* —
simple, descriptive, goes well with music of all sorts.
Millions of dollars invested in human resources
and ad campaigns to get this point across. And,
I admit, quite effective. I still remember growing up:
McDonald's is a happy place and *You deserve a break today.*

This is my story and the story of others without
marketing potential walking around hoping for
a moment or two when something about our lives
is different or exciting, hoping to get a picture
in the paper or on T.V. We are the normal majority
with limited investment potential. The kind
that responds to marketing hyperactivity because,
at least in print, it's inviting.

Better than what we face walking out the door. Better
than staring at our names on today's mail and asking:
Who cares? Better to eat hope than search for it.
Better to pay for it than believe in ourselves.

I cut up another mouthful and focus on the carry-out
bag on my table. The phrase is handsomely printed
in international languages. I keep staring, as if looking
at the words long enough might make them come true.

3 PM PACIFIC DAYLIGHT TIME

Across the world time is different.

6 PM in New York.
11 PM in London.
6 AM in Bangkok.
9 AM in Sydney.

I assume that today in my town
is every day but each step
east or west changes my perspective.
Time is what you gain or lose.

What time is it? someone asks.

Lunch time in Honolulu.
Breakfast in Tokyo.
Midnight love in Paris.

Time enough to spend it freely.
Not enough to pay it back.

MIDDAY STROLL

The morning sky is so azure.
Walking home, I cannot tell
if I'm being seduced or coerced.
All I know is that I'd like to fly
straight up and be comforted
or swallowed but I'm here,
two feet solid and plodding,
bereft, against swollen faces,
and broken bottles; against
vacancy and trash.

Is this the jest of creation?
To make the earth a jewel
and man its gargoyle?
Do we now stand pitted
as criminals against grace?

The wind blows off my questions.
The atmosphere is implacable,
an ocean of knowledge and art.
It rolls past my eyes,
flows across my face,
and bleeds into my arteries.
Will it be enough to save me?

WEATHER WEIRD

Scientists are concerned. Drought in Europe.
Tornadoes in Texas. Hurricanes in Brazil.

Global warming has finally caught us,
like a giant chemistry set declaring war.
If there is any doubt who is in charge,
ask these 250 mph twisters.

For years the earth has been our plow ox.
Now it seems the ox is let loose.
No more yoke. No more furrows.

Look at us now watching the weather
without any sign of an ark.
Wind and water everywhere.
The ghost of Noah growing impatient.

We see it all with our hands tied,
our own witches brew boiling over
while the alchemists frantically
experiment with artificial rainbows.

IRAQI PROTESTER NEXT TO BURNED BODIES ON A BRIDGE

He is right to scream.
What he perceives is not far from the truth.
The power of evil invading.
The corruption of righteousness.

I myself am not far from him though I doubt
he would believe it.

Would that I could wave a gun and give
his universe order.
The kind he shouts for.
The kind worth killing and burning soldiers,
journalists, anyone western.

What he does not see
what I have failed to notice until now:
How we eat our own, rebirth them,
then eat again.

He is right to scream.
If killing me would change his life
I might volunteer.

But his rage and mine — so convenient.
Blood, a river in our world, born to be shed
and we as tributaries doing what comes natural.

If there is a boat leaving, I have not found it.
I am simply swirling as he is, downstream,
toward the wide human gulf of voraciousness.

LESSONS LEARNED

In school today a boy on the Pakistan border
learns the benefits of hating Americans. His mother
and father killed in Kabul, a cousin resisting in Fallujah,
he is eager to grow up and get his own taste of flesh.
Both his rifle and hate feel good and he is just old enough
to wet himself over virgins.

In school today a young soldier at Ft. Bliss learns
tactics for killing the enemy. He remembers Lori Piestewa,
fallen comrades in Afghanistan, has several of his buddies
running raids around Fallujah. He feels a small tingle at
the thought of shooting an Iraqi in the head and of the
beer and pussy he'll get tonight.

As fate may have it, they could meet in battle.
As fate may have it, they could both be right. Fate,
I suspect, may be less willing to help them admit
they could also be wrong.

SURVIVAL

I don't expect a walnut to have the same shell
as a pecan or acorn. Every peculiar seed,
bush, and tree bears its own fruit.

Strange how humans expect differently.
As if all nuts, however odd and strangely flavored,
should hang from the same tree.

All my life, I have lived by this, believing that
people can be grafted, that every individual
has the same trunk.

Perhaps there are similarities, enough to fool us
but the plans for extermination tell us different;
the rational, determined intent of assassins.

It is the right of a wilderness to chaotically reproduce
and fight for sustenance. The order of this is clear.
What is not clear is our own mind.

Different trees and forests bearing seeds and nuts
with weapons and words and the will to war
living as if all of this is perfectly natural.

Who's to tell us we're not correct?

HOW TO GET AWAY WITH MURDER

The secret to injustice
is to not know.
Create separate chains
so that the top
doesn't see the bottom.
A child in the fields.
A prostitute.
A business bribe.
A gang drive-by.

The secret to blood-letting
is to not know.
Create separate sides
so that right and left
never touch fingers.
Believe all the pictures.
Chant the catch-phrase.
Talk only to yourselves.
Kill without question.

No knowledge.
No responsibility.
It really is that easy.
The earth turns
and brings day and night.
The earth turns
and brings unresolved grief.
Like the earth's rotation,
I understand the science.
I don't need to know the details.

PICTURES OF WAR

Defend, if you will, the honor of humanity.
Tell me how you see us as a higher species.
I will simply show you the film.
Here for all to see, our broadcast horror.

Oh how the machines rattle with publicity!
A burned body here. A mutilation there.
A chant about God and glory.
The champagne of retaliation.

I am thinking the real instigator,
the one pushing our throttles
like a seasoned pilot, has yet to surface.

He will soon. The fuse in place. The clock
ticking. The pieces laid out on the board.
In the crosshairs now, his rancorous grin,
the look of a mad bomber who knew all along
we could not resist the smell of bones.

CHICKAMAUGA REVISITED

The cars roll
between Georgia and Tennessee
but at Chickamauga,
all movement has ceased.

I came once
when I was young
and didn't listen.

Today is different.
As the armor rolls,
already in the works
more Chickamaugas,
more bodies,
more monuments,

but always,
safe out of sight,
the same death.

BRIEF MUSINGS FROM THE GETTY[1]

I. *Starry Night* by Edvard Munch

Blue strokes shimmering with tiny eyes
as if angels become more apparent in the dark.
I can only hope for enough faith to help them
playfully flutter off the canvas.

II. *Wheatstacks, Snow Effects Morning* by Claude Monet

Guessing that God passes early,
Monet waits to catch a glimpse.
Impressed by his persistence,
God smiles and sugars the fields;
throws on icing as an afterthought.

III. *Irises* by Vincent van Gogh

Most days he probes flowers
harmlessly looking for keyholes.
Not many notice how he waits
for the right moment to pick the lock
and make a mad dash for heaven.

IV. *A Walk At Dusk* by Caspar David Friedrich

Near the stone in half-light,
he presses the rock just enough
to know the ground is alive.
If only for an instant,
he can see, with head bowed,
there is no death, only surrender.

---

[1] For additional information and viewing of these paintings
see *www.getty.edu*

V. *The Entombment* by Peter Paul Rubens

From the wall, blood oozing.
They have come but not to see him carried out.
What now? The problem, like his body, is heavy.
A witness shakes her head.

VI. *Saint Bartholomew* by Rembrandt

Stares at me pensively and wonders,
for such a curious person, if I'll catch on.
He seems unsure. So many strange faces
coming and going. Who will be the exception?
I wait for a sign. He waits for my question.

AYERS ROCK, AUSTRALIA

When the earth emerged
like a cake from the oven,
I imagine it first rose here.

After Adam was banished,
before the flood tore everything to pieces,
Aborigines came to debate his errors.

When the Tower of Babel toppled,
as civilizations rose and crumbled,
the monolith sought seclusion.

The ocean has receded.
We are now convulsing in distant cities.
Only small traces of life within view.
The rock, however, still vigilant.

Through genocide and homicide.
Through nuclear waste and trash.
Through Armageddon and Antichrist.

The first and the last.
Where the Spirit holds court.
Red as a heart and still beating.

OCEAN VIEW

I think God came from the ocean.

The scriptures say that in the beginning
the Spirit of God was hovering over the waters[2]

but who can tell if these waters were also
the house, the living room, the bed,
when the earth was tumultuous
and God had nowhere else to go.

The ocean remains omnipresent.
Watching me as I lean on this rail.
The land has been infested
and we have grown like roaches
but out in the caves and bottoms,
the great low mountains and forests,
God still finds dark and rest.
With the whales and plankton.
With odd creatures of the trenches.
With rusted hulks and sailors' remains.

Perhaps at this moment, as I listen to
the foam tumble, God and angels
entertain themselves by roiling waves.
Perhaps someday in their exclusive estate
I may even be invited to visit.

----

[2] Genesis 1:2

LANDSCAPES BY ZHENG BAI ZHONG

Oh Mother and Father!
I have traveled too far too fast
and nothing in view feels familiar.
Even the language seems foreign.
True enough, there is a difference
in what I dream and what I live.
There is that long dirt path
that has no beginning or end.
Yet everything I have is in common
like a seed to the soil or air in the sky.
A man knows when he is lost or found.
I am neither. I know the distance from here
to there, and I know the who.
Now, if you would help me,
I am ready to come back.
Back to my country.
Back to my people.
Back to the source of my paint and paper.
Back to the soul of my artist.
One step at a time until
my feet fall into this river
and your sympathetic eyes sweep me up
to the very top of my snow-crest home.

www.ingramcontent.com/pod-product-compliance
Lightning Source LLC
Chambersburg PA
CBHW052226150726
48002CB00003B/1295